True Horse Stories

A Dolch Classic Basic Reading Book

by Edward W. Dolch and Marguerite P. Dolch

illustrated by Meryl Henderson

The Basic Reading Books

The Basic Reading Books are fun reading books that fill the need for easy-to-read stories for the primary grades. The interest appeal of these true stories will encourage independent reading at the early reading levels.

The stories focus on the 95 Common Nouns and the Dolch 220 Basic Sight Vocabulary. Beyond these simple lists, the books use about two or three new words per page.

This series was prepared under the direction and supervision of Edward W. Dolch, Ph.D.

This revision was prepared under the direction and supervision of Eleanor Dolch LaRoy and the Dolch Family Trust.

SRA/McGraw-Hill

*A Division of The **McGraw·Hill** Companies*

Printed in the United States of America.

Send all inquiries to:
SRA/McGraw-Hill
250 Old Wilson Bridge Road, Suite 310
Worthington, OH 43085

ISBN 0-02-830803-4

1 2 3 4 5 6 7 8 9 0 BUX 04 03 02 01 00 99 98

Table of Contents

A Smart Cow Pony

A cowhand needs a good cow pony to ride, but not every horse will be a good cow pony. A cow pony is not a very big horse. It is sometimes very wild. When a person tries to ride it, a cow pony sometimes bucks. It bucks and bucks. That is, it tries to throw the person off its back. A person must know a lot about horses to train a cow pony.

Brown Jug was a very smart cow pony. At first he did not want anyone to ride him, but a good cowhand trained him. The cowhand talked to the horse just as if the horse were another person. He told the cow pony that a good horse has to learn to work. A good cow pony has to learn to work with a person on its back.

Brown Jug stood still. He even let the friendly man put a saddle on his back. But when the man got into the saddle—how Brown Jug bucked. He bucked and bucked. But the man stayed on his back.

Day after day, that man put the saddle on Brown Jug's back. He always talked to the horse in a friendly way. It seemed that it did not help. When the man got in the saddle, Brown Jug bucked. But the man stayed on Brown Jug's back.

One day when the saddle was put on, Brown Jug bucked. The man pulled the rope on the horse's head in a way that threw Brown Jug to the ground.

Before Brown Jug knew what had happened, the cowhand tied Brown Jug's feet together.

Then the cowhand sat on Brown Jug and talked to him. The cowhand talked to Brown Jug for a long time. At last he let Brown Jug get up.

That day Brown Jug let the cowhand ride him. The little horse tried to do what the man wanted him to do.

Brown Jug was learning to be a good cow pony. But always, when the cowhand got on Brown Jug, he bucked just a little to show what he could do. Then he went about his work.

The work of a cow pony is very hard. It has to learn to make the cows go the way the cowhand wants them to go. Many times the cows want to go just the way they want to go.

Then too, the cow pony has to learn to get just one cow away from the other cows and make it go through a gate. The cowhand tells the cow pony which cow he wants. The cow pony understands. It goes right in among the cows and gets that one cow away from the other cows. This is called "cutting out" a cow.

Brown Jug became a very good cow pony. One day he showed what a smart

horse he was. The cowhand and Brown Jug were cutting out a great big cow from the other cows. This big cow was angry, and she did not want to go the way the cowhand and Brown Jug wanted her to go.

The big cow went the way she wanted to go, and Brown Jug headed her off. Then the big cow started to run back to the other cows. The cow pony had to run very fast and stop suddenly, then turn and run very fast the other way to keep her away from the other cows.

All at once, Brown Jug stepped in a hole in the ground. Over he went, and the cowhand fell off his back.

Brown Jug knew that he had to get that big cow away from the other cows. He got to his feet. He did not need a cowhand to tell him what to do. He went after the cow all by himself. He got the cow away from the other cows. He made that cow go through the gate.

How the cowhand laughed. He patted Brown Jug and said, "If there were more cow ponies like you, Brown Jug, we would not need to have cowhands."

Joe, the Cowhand

Joe was a young man who could ride a horse as well as any cowhand. A friend asked him to help drive a herd of wild horses.

"Come on over," said Mr. Henry, "and I will give you a good horse to ride. We need all the help we can get to drive the herd of wild horses."

"That is just what I would like to do," said Joe. So Joe went with Mr. Henry.

The next day, the cowhands went to the corral to get their riding horses. Mr. Henry showed Joe a horse on the far side of the corral.

"There is your horse, Joe," said Mr. Henry. "He is not as young as he used to be, but you will never ride a better horse."

Joe did not know what to think when he saw the horse. He had never seen such a horse. The other horses were running around the corral. The cowhands were catching them. Joe's horse just stood still. He let Joe walk right up to him. He let Joe put the saddle on his back, and then the horse stood still with his head hanging almost to the ground. Joe's horse looked as if he did not care about anything.

When Joe got on his horse, he found that it was a very good riding horse. He followed Mr. Henry and the other cowhands out to where the herd of wild horses were kept.

The long drive over the grass country started. The wild horses went slowly, eating the grass along the way. The cowhands kept watch. They did not want the horses to be frightened.

Day after day, the cowhands rode slowly along. It was very hot. The country changed. The grass country became country covered with brush and small trees. There was a road through the brush.

Joe and two other cowhands were riding down the road among the wild horses. Suddenly, they heard a noise ahead of them. The horses heard the noise, too. They lifted their heads. The wild horses ahead of Joe became frightened. The frightened horses left the road and rushed into the brush.

"We must get those horses back to the road before the other wild horses are frightened," called one of the cowhands, and they rode right into the brush after the frightened horses.

Joe did not see how a horse could get through the brush. He did not know what to do, but Joe's horse knew what to do. He went into the brush right after the cowhands. It was all Joe could do to stay on his horse.

Joe's horse knew that he must get the frightened horses back to the road. He got through the brush. Sometimes he backed through the brush. Sometimes he did little jumps to make his way through. The brush hurt Joe and the brush hurt the horse. They were both scratched and bleeding.

The next thing Joe knew, he had left the other cowhands behind. His horse was through the brush and in an open place. There were wild horses all around them. Joe thought that he was going to be hurt. But Joe's horse knew what to do.

Joe's horse ran ahead of the frightened wild horses. He made the first horse turn around. As the first horse turned, the other wild horses followed him.

Then Joe heard the other cowhands. They had come out of the brush into the open. They helped get the wild horses back to the road. Joe's horse knew just how to help.

At last the wild horses were together. They found a place beside the road where there was grass. The horses ate grass and the cowhands rested.

Joe looked at his horse. His horse was scratched and bleeding. He was not a nice-looking horse, but Joe thought he was the most beautiful horse that he had ever seen.

As Joe was trying to take care of his bleeding horse, he heard the other cowhands talking.

"That new man, Joe, is a good cowhand, and that horse of his is a fast horse. He got to those wild horses before we did and had almost turned them. That new man is a good cowhand."

Joe said into his horse's ear, "You did it all, old boy. I just went along for the ride."

Old Red

The cowhands in Texas like to tell about Old Red.

Every year, the cowhands rode into the brush. They rounded up the cows and the calves. The calves were branded so that people would know who owned them.

Each year the cowhands saw a big, red steer, but no cowhand ever got a rope over the long horns of this red steer. The cowhands called this steer Old Red.

Old Red knew just where to go. No cowhand was ever going to rope him and drive him in.

Cowhands cannot get cows and their calves out of the brush without the help of their cow ponies. Cow ponies are small horses. They are very smart horses. They can run very fast, and they can stop suddenly.

When a cowhand gets a rope over the horns of the cow, the cow pony suddenly stops and pulls back hard. The cow falls to the ground. The cowhand jumps down, runs to the cow, and ties its feet together. At the same time, the cow pony is pulling on the rope so the cow cannot get up.

One night, there was a big moon. The cowhands thought they would round up some of the cows in the moonlight. Very quietly, they rode through the brush. They found a few cows eating grass in the moonlight, and with the cows was a big, red steer.

The cowhands threw their ropes. They roped many of the cows, and one cowhand got his rope over the horns of the big, red steer just as it ran into the brush. The cow pony stopped suddenly, but he did not throw the steer.

The cow pony pulled on the rope. The steer pulled on the rope. Then the big, red steer turned in the brush and rushed at the cow pony. The cowhand saw that the steer was Old Red.

When Old Red rushed the cow pony, he went around a small tree. He rushed the pony but got to the end of the rope that was around the tree. The sudden stop threw Old Red around so that his back end hit the pony.

The cowhand got the steer's tail and pulled as hard as he could. Then he called for help with all his might.

The other cowhands rode up. They got their ropes on Old Red. They threw him down, and they tied him to the tree.

How the cowhands laughed when they told about Old Red. Old Red, the steer that no one could catch, had been caught by the tail.

Tommy, the Rosinback

Have you ever gone to the circus and seen a beautiful woman dance on the back of a horse? Maybe you saw Tommy.

Tommy was a beautiful white horse. He knew just what to do so that the woman who danced on his back would not fall off.

In the circus, Tommy is called a "rosinback." A rosinback is a horse on which people in the circus do tricks. A rosinback must be a light-colored horse so that the rosin on his back does not show. Rosin keeps the trick rider from falling.

A rosinback must be trained with care. Each time the horse goes around the circus ring, it must take the same number of steps. When a person is jumping on and off the horse's back, that horse must be where the rider wants it to be.

When a rosinback is in the ring, it must not change its steps, no matter what goes on around it. The horse must keep going around the circus ring in just the same number of steps.

There was once a big wind that blew a circus tent away. The rosinback was in the circus ring going around and around. When the tent blew away, the horse kept going around the ring just as though nothing had happened.

When Tommy first went to the circus, no one thought that he could be trained to be a rosinback. Tommy did not like men, and he would not let anyone ride on his back.

John got Tommy for the circus because Tommy was such as beautiful horse. Tommy was wild and would not let anyone ride him. Tommy would not even let John touch him.

Ella was watching Tommy. She was the woman who danced on the back of a horse. She loved horses. She had always trained her rosinbacks.

"That horse is afraid of men," Ella said. "I know that some men have been very bad to him. Let me see whether I can make friends with him."

"I am afraid that Tommy is a bad horse," said John. "I am afraid that he will hurt you."

Ella got some sugar. "You go where Tommy cannot see you," said Ella. "I am going to make friends with Tommy."

John went behind a circus tent and he watched. Very slowly, Ella went closer to Tommy. All the time, she was talking to him.

"Come on, Tommy," said Ella. "I am not going to hurt you. I have something that you will like to eat. Come on, Tommy, I am your friend. I will not hurt you."

Tommy lifted his ears. He seemed to like this soft voice. He liked to have this lady talk to him. He did not run away. The lady did not try to touch him. She held out her hand, and in her hand was something that Tommy wanted to eat.

It was a long time before Tommy ate the sugar from Ella's hand. All the time, she was talking to him in her soft voice. Not once did she make the horse afraid by trying to touch him.

The next morning, Tommy took something to eat from Ella's hand. This time, Tommy lifted his soft nose up to Ella as if to thank her. But when Ella lifted up her other hand to touch Tommy on the head, Tommy became afraid and ran away.

"All right," said Ella. "You don't want to be my friend right now. I am going away."

Ella turned her back on Tommy and did not look at him. She did not talk to him in her soft voice. She just stood very still with her back to the horse.

Pretty soon, Tommy went to her. He looked around to see whether she had some sugar in her hand, but she did not stay and talk to him.

"Good-bye, Tommy," said Ella. "I am going away." Ella walked away, and she did not look back.

Tommy went to the fence and watched Ella. He wanted Ella to come back.

The next morning, Ella fed Tommy. The big horse let her brush him. He put his head down so that she could pat him.

Ella talked to Tommy about the saddle. She showed him the saddle and let him smell it. At last, Tommy let Ella put the saddle on his back. He let Ella get up in the saddle and ride him around. He held his head up. He put his feet down with care as if he were trying not to hurt this lady.

From that time on, Tommy would do anything that Ella asked. It was not long before Tommy became her rosinback in the circus ring. She danced on his back, and Tommy was very careful not to hurt Ella.

Once Buffalo Bill wanted to buy Tommy. He said that he would give Ella as much money as she asked for Tommy. But Ella said, "I cannot sell Tommy. I cannot sell one of my friends, and Tommy and I are friends."

Mother Goose

Most horses don't like elephants. They are afraid of those great animals. But in a circus, all kinds of animals are together. They have to get used to one another.

Mother Goose was an old horse. She liked elephants, and elephants liked her. The man who looked after the elephants rode Mother Goose, and where Mother Goose went, the elephants followed.

One time the circus elephants ran away out into the country. They broke down fences and pulled up small trees. The people were afraid of the elephants because they were so big.

The man who looked after the elephants got on Mother Goose. He rode out into the country. When the elephants saw Mother Goose, they did not run away. They liked Mother Goose.

The man rode back to the circus. All of the elephants followed Mother Goose. Each elephant went to its place in the elephant tent, and the circus men chained them in their places.

Mother Goose was getting very old. She got very tired walking ahead of the elephants in the circus parade.

So, they put Mother Goose in a horse tent. She had a nice place to sleep. She did not have to take care of the elephants. But Mother Goose was not happy, and the elephants were not happy.

Every night, one of the big elephants pulled up its chain and went to the horse tent to see Mother Goose. The elephants even tried to get into the horse tent and sleep beside Mother Goose. Sometimes two or three elephants went to the horse tent and tried to sleep beside Mother Goose.

The other horses in the horse tent did not like the elephants, and the elephants did not like the other horses. Such a noise at night you never heard!

There was only one thing to do, and that was to let Mother Goose sleep in the elephant tent. And that is why you might see an old horse sleeping in the elephant tent. The horse was too old to work, but she kept the elephants happy.

The man who looks after the elephants always says, "A happy elephant is a good elephant."

Tony, Who Thought for Himself

Tony was a beautiful palomino horse, and Tony was a circus horse.

One day, Derrick was sitting beside a road in the country. He was talking to a friend. The two men, who both loved horses, were talking about the right way to train a horse. Derrick had trained many circus horses.

"You watch what a horse does," said Derrick. "Many horses shake their heads up and down when flies are around them. I give a horse some sugar when it shakes its head up and down. Soon it knows that I want it to shake its head up and down. Each time I do this, I hold my hand in the same way. Soon when I hold my hand this way, the horse will shake its head up and down. Then I can ask it anything. It shakes its head up and down, and people think that the horse is saying 'Yes.'"

Just then the two men heard a horse on the road. It was a beautiful palomino horse with a long, white tail. Derrick knew at once that he must have that horse.

The man who was riding Tony said he would sell him to Derrick, and Derrick took the palomino to the circus.

Derrick knew that he had a very beautiful horse for his circus. Then when he started to train Tony, he found that Tony was the best horse that he had ever tried to train.

Most circus horses do their tricks the same way every time they go into the circus ring, but Tony could think for himself. He changed his tricks when he wanted to.

Tony and Derrick had a trick that always made children laugh. Derrick said to Tony, "Funnyface, why don't you do what I tell you to do?"

Tony acted as if he were very angry at being called Funnyface. He ran Derrick all around the circus ring.

Then Derrick called out to Tony, "Beautiful, beautiful, you are not a funnyface." Then Tony lifted his nose up to Derrick's ear and seemed to talk to him.

At the end of the act, Tony ran Derrick out of the circus ring. Derrick had to run fast or Tony would catch him. Then Tony went back all by himself and bowed to the people.

Tony loved the circus. He liked to do his tricks. But there was one thing that Tony did not like to do. Tony did not like to work the way other horses do.

One day Derrick's friend wanted to get a little wagon that he had left at a farm. He needed a horse to pull the wagon. Derrick told his friend, "Take Tony. Ride him to the farm. He can pull your wagon back to the circus. It will do Tony good to get out into the country."

So the friend put a saddle on Tony and rode him out into the country to the farm. He took the saddle off Tony and put it into the wagon. Then he hitched Tony to the wagon. But Tony would not pull the wagon. He just stood still.

The friend knew that Tony would not do anything he did not want to do. So, the friend left Tony at the farm and took the train back to the circus. He got another horse and rode him out to the farm.

He hitched the other horse to the wagon. Then he tied Tony to the back of the wagon and started out for the circus. But Tony bit the rope he was tied with. He did not want to be tied to a wagon.

The man saw what he must do. He started back to the circus in the wagon. Tony followed along behind. When Tony wanted to, he stopped and ate the green grass beside the road. Then he caught up with the wagon. He did not run away. He knew he was to go with the wagon, but he was not going to be tied to the wagon.

The man, the wagon, Tony, and the other horse got back to the circus. Tony, who thought for himself, had had a good time in the country. Tony would work hard doing his tricks, but he would not work like other horses and pull a wagon.

The Old, White Horse

Charley was just an old, white horse, but he was happy because he had work to do. He worked at a factory.

Everyday Mr. Dooley took the old, white horse to the yard of the factory. In the yard stood a big pole with a big wheel on the top of it. Mr. Dooley hitched Charley to a small pole that turned the big pole. As the big pole turned, the wheel at the top went round and round.

All day long Charley walked around and around the big pole. As he walked around, he pulled the small pole that turned the big pole that turned the big wheel. The big wheel was fixed so that it turned some wheels in the factory.

All year long, Charley walked around and around in the factory yard. In the rain and in the sun, Charley worked every day, and Charley liked his work.

When the factory whistle blew in the morning, the people started to work in the factory. And Charley started to work in the factory yard. When the factory whistle blew again, the people in the factory stopped to eat. And Mr. Dooley took Charley something to eat, too.

When the factory whistle blew for people to stop their work for the day, Charley stopped his work. Mr. Dooley took the old, white horse back home. Charley was very happy with his work at the factory.

But one day Mr. Dooley got a young, black horse. He hitched the black horse to a wagon. He tied Charley to the back of the wagon. Charley did not know what was going to happen.

Mr. Dooley got into the wagon. He did not go to the factory yard. He went out into the country where the grass was green. At last he stopped and untied Charley from the back of the wagon. He opened a gate and put Charley into a green pasture.

Charley went into the pasture and stood there. He did not know what to do.

"Charley, my boy," said Mr. Dooley, "you are going to have a fine time. All day long you can eat the green grass. You will not have to work. And I will come to see you and bring you a red apple."

Mr. Dooley got into the wagon and went back to the factory.

For a long time, Charley stood just where Mr. Dooley had left him. Charley was not happy. Every now and then he lifted his head. He wanted to hear the noise of the factory.

After a time, Charley ate some green grass and found that it was very good. When the sun got hot, the old horse went and stood under a tree that was in the pasture.

The grass was very good and the sun was warm. But Charley, the old, white horse, was not happy. He had no work to do.

Very soon Charley did not even want to eat the green grass. The old horse began to look tired and sick.

Then one day, the wind blew from the factory to the pasture. Charley's head went up. He heard the factory whistle. Charley walked right to the tree that was in the pasture. He began to

walk around and around the tree, just as
he had walked around and around the
big pole in the factory yard.

All morning Charley walked around
the tree. The old, white horse was very
happy. When he heard the whistle again,
Charley stopped walking around the
tree. He ate some of the grass in the
pasture. He went down to the little river
and had a drink of water. Everything
was so good because Charley had worked
all morning.

Then he heard the whistle that called the people at the factory back to work. Charley went right back to the tree that was in the pasture. He walked around and around the tree. He did not stop until he heard the whistle that told the people at the factory that it was time to go home.

Then Charley ran and jumped about. He played in the pasture just like a young horse. And when he was tired of running and jumping, he ate the green grass and went to sleep.

Charley knew what to do. Even when the wind did not blow from the factory so that Charley could hear the whistle, Charley went to work. Every morning he walked around and around the tree in the pasture. And after he had stopped to eat, he again walked around and around the tree in the pasture.

Charley, the old, white horse, was happy. Every day he had his work to do.

The Circus Fire

Bill thought that Skippy was the most brave horse he had ever heard of. Bill was a police officer. He rode Skippy up and down the streets of a big city. One day Skippy showed Bill what a brave horse he was.

Bill was riding Skippy down the street. Skippy threw up his head. Then Bill smelled smoke. He heard the fire trucks coming down the street. He and Skippy went after the fire trucks.

Now there are two things that most horses are afraid of. They are afraid of fire, and they are afraid of elephants.

As Bill and Skippy were riding to the fire, many people were in the street.

"The circus is on fire," cried the people. "The circus is on fire."

Then Skippy saw ten big elephants.
They were coming right at him.

"Skippy, you are all right," said Bill.
"The elephants will not hurt you."

Skippy began to shake all over, but
he did not run away.

The elephant keeper was leading the
elephants away from the fire. They went

by Skippy, very close to him. Each elephant held the tail of the elephant in front. Some of the elephants had been hurt in the fire, but the elephants had done just what the keeper wanted them to do, and they were saved from the fire.

"Good boy, Skippy," said Bill. "You did not run away from the elephants. Let us get to the fire. Maybe we can help."

The tents of the circus were burning. There were animals and people running all about. Bill was glad that the show had not started because fathers and mothers and children were not there.

Bill and Skippy went into the tent where the horses were kept. They smelled lots of smoke. The tent was full of smoke. The horses were afraid. They were running around. They would not do what their keepers wanted them to do.

The tent started to burn. The keepers had to get the horses out of the tent or they would all be burned.

"We must help get the horses out of the tent, Skippy. Go in, boy," said Bill. "Go into the tent."

Skippy was afraid of the fire. He was shaking all over.

"Go in, Skippy," said Bill. "Go into the tent." And Skippy went into the burning tent.

A man called to Bill, "Get the white horse. The white horse leads the parade. If you get the white horse to go out of the tent, the other horses will follow it."

"Skippy," said Bill, "get the white horse. Get the white horse."

The white horse was running around and around with the other horses. The horses were kicking each other. Some horses' manes and tails were burning. The horses were so afraid that they did not know what they were doing.

The tent was getting so full of smoke that Bill and Skippy could hardly see.

Bill rode Skippy in among the kicking and biting horses. He could just see the white horse.

At last Bill got hold of the rope that was on the head of the white horse. He pulled and pulled. Skippy started to lead the white horse out of the door of the tent. Then the other horses in the burning tent followed the white horse out.

The people who were watching saw a strange circus parade. A police officer rode a brown horse that was pulling a white horse that was badly frightened. And behind the white horse came many badly frightened circus horses. Their manes and tails were burned, but they followed the white horse, just as they did in the circus parade.

a
about
act
acted
afraid
after
again
ahead
all
almost
along
always
am
among
an
and
angry
animals
another
any
anyone
anything
apple
are
around
as
ask
asked
at
ate
away
back
backed
bad
badly
be
beautiful

became
because
been
before
began
behind
being
beside
best
better
big
Bill
bit
black
bleeding
blew
blow
both
bowed
boy
branded
brave
bring
broke
brown
brush
bucked
bucks
Buffalo
burn
burned
burning
but
buy
by
called
calves

came
can
cannot
care
careful
catch
catching
caught
chain
chained
change
changed
Charley
Charley's
children
circus
city
close
closer
colored
come
coming
corral
could
country
covered
cow
cowhand
cowhands
cows
cried
cutting
dance
danced
day
Derrick
Derrick's

did
do
does
doing
done
don't
Dooley
door
down
drink
drive
each
ear
ears
eat
eating
elephant
elephants
Ella
Ella's
end
even
ever
every
everyday
everything
factory
fall
falling
falls
far
farm
fast
fathers
fed
feet
fell

fence
fences
few
fine
fire
first
fixed
flies
follow
followed
for
found
friend
friendly
friends
frightened
from
front
full
Funnyface
gate
get
gets
getting
give
glad
go
goes
going
gone
good
good-bye
goose
got
grass
great
green

ground
had
hand
hanging
happen
happened
happy
hard
hardly
has
have
he
head
headed
heads
hear
heard
held
help
helped
Henry
her
herd
him
himself
his
hit
hitched
hold
hole
home
horns
horse
horses
horse's
horses'
hot

how
hurt
I
if
in
into
is
it
its
Joe
Joe's
John
Jug
Jug's
jumped
jumping
jumps
just
keep
keeper
keepers
keeps
kept
kicking
kinds
knew
know
knows
lady
last
laugh
laughed
lead
leads
learn
learning
left

let
lifted
light
like
liked
little
long
look
looked
looking
looks
lot
loved
made
make
man
manes
many
matter
maybe
me
men
might
money
moon
moonlight
more
morning
most
mother
mothers
Mr.
much
must
my
need
needed

needs
never
new
next
nice
night
no
noise
nose
not
nothing
now
number
of
off
officer
old
on
once
one
only
open
opened
or
other
out
over
owned
palomino
parade
pasture
pat
patted
people
person
place
places

played
pole
police
ponies
pony
pretty
pull
pulled
pulling
pulls
put
quietly
rain
ran
red
rested
ride
rider
riding
right
ring
river
road
rode
rope
roped
ropes
rosin
rosinback
rosinbacks
round
rounded
run
running
runs
rushed
saddle

said
same
sat
saved
saw
saying
says
scratched
see
seemed
seen
sell
shake
shakes
shaking
she
show
showed
sick
side
sitting
Skippy
sleep
sleeping
slowly
small
smart
smell
smelled
smoke
so
soft
some
something
sometimes
soon
started

stay
stayed
steer
steer's
stepped
steps
still
stood
stop
stopped
stops
strange
street
streets
such
sudden
suddenly
sugar
sun
tail
tails
take
talk
talked
talking
tell
tells
ten
tent
tents
Texas
thank
that
the
their
them
then

there
these
they
thing
things
think
this
those
though
thought
three
threw
through
throw
tied
ties
time
times
tired
to
together
told
Tommy
Tony
too
took
top
touch
train
trained
tree
trees
trick
tricks
tried
tries
trucks

try
trying
turn
turned
two
under
understands
untied
until
up
us
used
very
voice
wagon
walk
walked
walking
want
wanted
wants
warm
was
watch
watched
watching
water
way
we
well
went
were
what
wheel
wheels
when
where

wherever
whether
which
whistle
white
who
why
wild
will
wind
with

without
woman
work
worked
would
yard
year
yes
you
young
your

DATE DUE

MAR 2 0 2002			
MAR 1 3 REC'D			
AUG 0 7 2004			
AUG 1 1 REC'D			
AUG 0 7 2009			
JUL 2 0 REC'D			
OCT 0 3 2010			
GAYLORD			PRINTED IN U.S.A.